W9-CQK-866

ROAD TO WAR
CAUSES OF CONFLICT

CAUSES
OF THE
CIVIL
WAR

ROAD TO WAR
CAUSES OF CONFLICT

ROAD TO WAR
CAUSES OF CONFLICT

CAUSES
OF THE
CIVIL
WAR

James F. Epperson

OTTN
PUBLISHING
STOCKTON, NJ

OTTN Publishing
16 Risler Street
Stockton, NJ 08859
www.ottnpublishing.com

Copyright © 2005 by OTTN Publishing. All rights reserved.
Printed and bound in the United States of America.

First printing

1 3 5 7 9 8 6 4 2

Library of Congress Cataloging-in-Publication Data

Epperson, James F.
  Causes of the Civil War / James F. Epperson.
    p. cm. — (The road to war)
  Summary: "Explains the causes of the American Civil War, includ-
ing legislative efforts to prevent the conflict, and the rising sectional
tensions during the 1850s that ultimately led to rebellion by the
Southern states"—Provided by publisher.
  Includes bibliographical references and index.
  ISBN-13: 978-1-59556-002-5 (hardcover)
  ISBN-10: 1-59556-002-5 (hardcover)
  ISBN-13: 978-1-59556-006-3 (pbk.)
  ISBN-10: 1-59556-006-8 (pbk.)
  1. United States—History—Civil War, 1861-1865—Causes—Juve-
nile literature. 2. United States—Politics and government—1849-
1861—Juvenile literature. I. Title. II. Series.
  E459.E66 2006
  973.7'11—dc22

                                          2005011100

Frontispiece: The bombardment of Fort Sumter, April 12, 1865.

TABLE OF CONTENTS

NOTABLE FIGURES

BROWN, JOHN (1800–1859). A radical abolitionist, Brown is remembered mainly for two infamous incidents: the 1855 massacre of five pro-slavery settlers near Pottawatomie Creek, in Kansas; and the October 1859 raid on the federal armory at Harpers Ferry, Virginia, which he hoped would spark a slave revolt.

BUCHANAN, JAMES (1791–1868). The 15th president of the United States is often criticized for his indecisiveness in dealing with the mounting secession crisis that ultimately led to the Civil War.

CALHOUN, JOHN C. (1782–1850). The opposition of his home state, South Carolina, to the federal tariffs of 1828 and 1832 inspired Calhoun to lay out the rationale for state nullification of a national law; for the rest of his political career Calhoun was an outspoken defender of Southern rights and the slavery system.

CLAY, HENRY (1777–1852). During his many terms in Congress, Clay earned the nickname "the Great Compromiser" for his central role in resolving the Missouri crisis, the nullification crisis, and the crisis of 1850.

DAVIS, JEFFERSON (1808–1889). A Mississippian who championed Southern rights, Davis served as secretary of war under President Franklin Pierce and as a U.S. senator before being chosen as president of the Confederate States of America in 1861.

DOUGLAS, STEPHEN A. (1813–1861). The senator from Illinois played a key role in the Compromise of 1850 and, with the Kansas-Nebraska Act of 1854, promoted

| John Brown | James Buchanan | John C. Calhoun |

popular sovereignty as a means of deciding whether new territories would be slave or free.

LINCOLN, ABRAHAM (1809–1865). The future 16th president of the United States rose to national prominence during the 1858 Illinois senatorial race against Stephen Douglas, when he eloquently argued against slavery; his election to the presidency in 1860 precipitated the secession of several Southern states and touched off the Civil War.

SCOTT, DRED (1795?–1858). A slave, Scott sued for his freedom, arguing that his being taken to free soil released him from bondage; the U.S. Supreme Court ruled against Scott in a controversial 1857 decision.

STOWE, HARRIET BEECHER (1811–1896). An abolitionist, Stowe wrote the 1852 novel *Uncle Tom's Cabin*, which helped solidify anti-slavery sentiment in the North.

TANEY, ROGER (1777–1864). As chief justice of the United States, Taney wrote the Supreme Court's decision in the case of *Dred Scott v. Sandford*; the decision asserted that blacks could not be citizens within the meaning of the U.S. Constitution and declared the Missouri Compromise unconstitutional.

TURNER, NAT (1800–1831). A slave and self-styled preacher, Turner led an August 1831 slave rebellion in Southampton County, Virginia, that claimed dozens of lives and produced fear and hysteria in the South.

SEEDS OF
CONFLICT

A slave dealer's office in Alexandria, Virginia. Slaves were kept in the low, windowless building to the left. The slave pictured below has a badly scarred back from being whipped. Slavery was a major underlying cause of the Civil War, which began in April 1861.

1

Early on the morning of April 12, 1861, a single shell was fired high over the harbor of Charleston, South Carolina. The shell, its fuse burning red in the darkness, reached the apex of its flight and began descending. Then it exploded over the water. This was a signal to soldiers manning cannons at different places around the harbor to open fire on Fort Sumter, an island stronghold held by U.S. soldiers.

The attack on Fort Sumter is considered the start of the American Civil War. This bloody conflict lasted until April 1865 and claimed more American lives—about 620,000—than any other war in history.

Disagreements between the Northern and Southern sections of the country had been building since the early 19th century, and they had become especially heated since 1850. Many complex issues contributed to the start of the war, including economic and social differences between North and South, attitudes about westward expansion, and the struggle for national political power. But underlying each of these issues was the major source of friction between the two sections: slavery.

SLAVERY IN AMERICA

By the 1700s, the institution of slavery was established in all 13 American colonies, though most slaves lived in the South. During the American Revolution (1775–1783), colonial leaders argued that all men are created equal and have a right to life, liberty, and the pursuit of happiness. Because of these high-minded principles, by the time the war ended some Americans were uncomfortable with slavery.

When the Constitutional Convention convened in Philadelphia in 1787, the issue of slavery divided the delegates. Some of the Northern delegates wanted the complete, immediate *abolition* of slavery. That was unacceptable to the Southern states. Eventually, the delegates agreed to a compromise. The Constitution would allow Congress to prohibit slaves from being imported into the country in 1808 (though the words *slavery* and *slave* do not actually appear in the Constitution).

Another controversy at the Constitutional Convention concerned how slaves would be considered by the national census. This was important because state population would determine the number of seats each state would have in the House of Representatives.

George Washington presides over the 1787 Constitutional Convention in Philadelphia. As delegates developed the basic framework by which the United States would be governed, they largely avoided dealing with the thorny question of slavery.

Northern Delegates said that only free men should be counted. This would favor the more populous Northern states. Southern delegates argued that slaves should be fully counted, which would give the South, with its large slave population, more congressional representation. In the end, a compromise was crafted: each slave would count as three-fifths of a person.

As delegates to the Constitutional Convention debated these questions, Congress passed the Northwest Ordinance. This act outlawed slavery in all of the territory north of the Ohio River and west of the Appalachian Mountains (the states of Ohio, Indiana, Illinois, Michigan, and Wisconsin, along with part of Minnesota, were formed from this area). Between the Northwest Ordinance and the Constitution's provision to end the slave trade, the Founding Fathers who opposed slavery had good reason to hope the institution would die out within a few years.

During the 1790s and early 1800s, most Northern states gradually abolished slavery. This did not occur in the South, however. Instead, the slave population expanded dramatically. In 1790, the first federal census counted nearly 690,000 slaves. By 1810, two years after Congress banned the importation of slaves, that number stood at 1.2 million. In 1830, the census counted more than 2 million slaves.

Slaves operate a cotton gin, a machine that could quickly and efficiently remove seeds from cotton bolls. Before 1793, cleaning a pound of cotton by hand took one day; the cotton gin could clean 50 pounds in the same time. As cotton became a profitable crop, more slaves were required to tend larger fields on Southern plantations.

The slave system flourished in the South because slaves were needed for agriculture. In the South, the land and climate were ideal for growing cotton, rice, sugar, and tobacco. The big plantations on which these *cash crops* were cultivated required a large source of cheap labor. These crops would not grow in the cooler Northern climate, so there was little economic incentive to maintain slavery in the North.

THE MISSOURI CRISIS

The first major issue in which slavery arose as an issue of sectional (that is, North-South) conflict

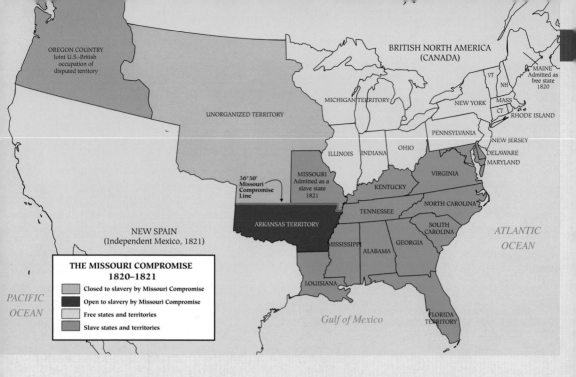

THE MISSOURI COMPROMISE
1820–1821

Closed to slavery by Missouri Compromise

Open to slavery by Missouri Compromise

Free states and territories

Slave states and territories

concerned the admission of Missouri as a state in 1820. Even though slavery existed in Missouri Territory, Congressman James Tallmadge of New York proposed that Missouri be admitted to the Union only as a non-slave state. His proposal passed in the House of Representatives, but failed in the Senate.

Unlike representation in the House, which is based on a state's population, each state sends two senators to Congress. Until 1820, there had been an equal number of slave and free states, so legislation could not pass the Senate unless it was acceptable to all. Senators from the South feared that adding more non-slave states would upset the balance of power. The free states of the North would be able to pass legislation without needing Southern cooperation or approval.

To settle the controversy, Maine was admitted as a free state, while Missouri was admitted as a slave state. It was then proposed that no more slave states would be created from the former Louisiana Territory north of the latitude line 36°30´—that is, north of Missouri's southern border. Congress passed this proposal in what came to be known as the Missouri Compromise. Along with the practice of admitting states in pairs—one slave, one free—the Missouri Compromise would be a guiding principle of national politics for more than 30 years.

THE NULLIFICATION CRISIS

The next major sectional crisis occurred in 1832. Congress had enacted steep *tariffs*, or taxes, on many imported goods in 1824, 1828, and 1832. The tariffs were intended not only to raise more revenue for the federal government, but also to help American factories compete against European manufacturers that could produce certain goods more cheaply. The tariffs helped factory owners in the Northern states, but hurt the Southern economy, which depended on trade with Europe. Farmers in the South and Midwest would pay higher prices for the goods they needed.

Opposition to the tariffs was strongest in South Carolina, the home state of the vice president, John C. Calhoun. At the behest of state leaders, Calhoun anonymously wrote a pair of essays that outlined a theory called *nullification*, under which a state legislature could invalidate an act of the U.S. Congress. South Carolina then enacted an "ordinance of nullification" in November 1832, declaring that the high tariffs were null and void—and the import duties would therefore not be collected—in the state.

President Andrew Jackson insisted that states could not nullify a law passed by Congress. He declared that, if necessary, he would send troops to collect the tariff. Meanwhile, Senator Henry Clay of Kentucky worked out a compromise tariff level that was acceptable to the South Carolinians. The nullification crisis passed. However, the question of states' rights versus federal authority had not been settled.

CHANGING ATTITUDES

In August 1831, a violent slave uprising occurred in Virginia's Southampton County. The rebellion, directed by Nat Turner, led to the deaths of 60 whites and 200 blacks. Most of the white victims were women and children. Turner's savage revolt caused Virginia to contemplate—but ultimately reject—a gradual *emancipation* act. Instead, Virginia tightened restrictions on blacks, slave as well as free. And elsewhere in the South, Nat Turner's rebellion provoked much fear among whites. Slaves in other states accused of involvement with Turner were executed.

In the North, attitudes toward slavery were changing. During the 1830s and 1840s, *abolitionist* groups like the American Anti-Slavery Society began to discuss the issue publicly. These groups wished to show Americans the moral injustices of slavery and completely eliminate the institution.

However, more Northerners opposed slavery for economic, rather than moral, reasons. As the American frontier moved west, farmers were encouraged to settle the fertile new territories. If those settlers were permitted to use slaves, they would be able to produce and sell their products more cheaply than farmers in the free North. At the same time, newly arrived immigrants employed in Northern factories feared they would lose their jobs to cheap slave labor.

In the South, a subtle change in attitude was also occurring. Historically, most Americans felt slavery was a "necessary evil" that had to be tolerated for the economic well-being of the South. By 1845, however, an important segment of the Southern population had begun to develop the idea that slavery was not a necessary evil, but a "positive good" that should be encouraged and expanded. This change of attitude was a key element in the drift toward civil war.

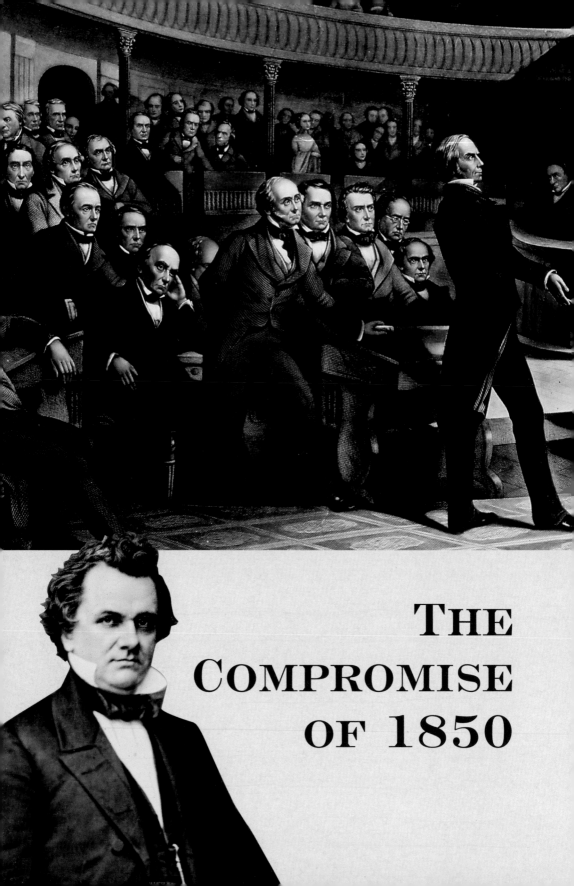

THE COMPROMISE OF 1850

Henry Clay, nicknamed "the Great Compromiser," introduces a bill in the U.S. Senate intended to prevent sectional warfare. Stephen Douglas (bottom left) played a key role in passing the legislation. Although the Compromise of 1850 succeeded in ending the immediate threat of war, it contributed to new tensions between North and South.

2

During the 1820s, a large number of Europeans and Americans immigrated to the region of Mexico known as Texas. There they set up a "colony" under the leadership of Stephen F. Austin. Initially, the Mexican government welcomed the new arrivals. But tensions soon arose, ultimately leading to the Texas Revolution of 1835–1836, in which Texas won its independence from Mexico. For nearly nine years afterward, Texas functioned as an independent nation. In 1845 it was *annexed* by the United States as a new slave state.

THE MEXICAN WAR

The Mexicans were not happy with this development. They had never completely accepted the independence of Texas, and there was some dispute about the border between Texas and Mexico. President James K. Polk offered Mexico a large sum of money to recognize the U.S. annexation of Texas, and a larger sum of money to *cede* to the United States the rest of northern Mexico, including the rich province of California. The overture was rejected and the two nations went to war, essentially over the disputed boundary, in May 1846.

On August 8, 1846, barely three months into the war, Congressman David Wilmot of Pennsylvania offered a resolution to the effect that any lands added to the United States as a result of the war with Mexico would not be allowed to have slavery. This became known as the Wilmot Proviso. It passed the House of Representatives twice, but never passed the Senate. Still, the Wilmot Proviso was significant because it marked the first time the idea had been advanced that no more U.S. territories should be opened to slavery.

In 1846, Pennsylvania congressman David Wilmot (1814–1868) introduced legislation that would have prevented the spread of slavery into Western territories gained through war with Mexico.

A new term began to appear in American politics: *Free-Soiler*. This label would be applied to someone who was not concerned with abolishing slavery where it already existed, but who opposed admitting any new slave states or organizing any new slave territories. The idea was that if no more slave states entered the Union, slavery would eventually die out. Another term that began to be used at about this time was *fire-eater*. This referred to Southern extremists who were vocally opposed to restrictions on slavery.

THE CALIFORNIA QUESTION

The Mexican War came to an end in 1848, with the victorious United States forcing Mexico to cede the territory that President Polk had offered to buy before the war began. In the long term, the United States would reap enormous benefits from acquiring the land, which would eventually become California, Nevada, Utah, Arizona, and New Mexico. But in the short term, the end of the Mexican War brought only a heightening of sectional tensions. Politicians in the North and South saw the huge new territory as a prize to be fought over.

The immediate problem was California. The territory was brimming with settlers, as gold had been discovered there in 1848. Enough people lived there to justify its admission into the Union, and the region was in desperate need of the kind of governmental authority that statehood would bring. But some Southern politicians vowed that their states would *secede* if California was admitted as a free state.

Ever since the Missouri crisis, Congress had admitted new states roughly in pairs, one free and one slave. This maintained the balance of power in the Senate. Thus Maine entered the Union in 1820 and Missouri in 1821; Arkansas in 1836 and Michigan in 1837; Florida in 1845 and Iowa in 1846; Texas in 1845 and Wisconsin in 1848. But in the immediate aftermath of the Mexican War, there was no obvious slave state waiting to be admitted into the Union.

Most of the new Californians were from free states, and slavery did not stand much chance of being established there. Yet the Southern fire-eaters refused to give up California. What was needed was a far-reaching and long-lasting settlement of the slavery question in all its aspects.

ANATOMY OF A COMPROMISE

In January 1850, Senator Henry Clay stepped forward to offer what became known as the Compromise of 1850. The provisions of Clay's bill included the admission of California as a free state; organization of Utah and New Mexico (including present-day Arizona) as territories without regard to the slavery question; the end of slave sales in the District of Columbia; a resolution that slavery in the District of Columbia would never be abolished without the consent of both the District and Maryland; a more effective fugitive slave law; and a resolution that Congress had no power to interfere with the interstate slave trade. Similar measures had already been introduced to Congress as separate bills. Clay's contribution was to lump them together and put his influence behind them all.

The bill faced an uncertain future. Many in Congress, at both ends of the political spectrum, could not in good conscience vote for some of the measures, and

President Zachary Taylor, from Clay's own Whig Party, opposed it.

Formal debate on the bill began in the Senate on May 13, 1850, and carried on throughout the summer. Supporters of the bill received an unexpected though tragic boost when President Taylor died in July; his successor, Millard Fillmore, was in favor of the compromise. But only about a third of either house of Congress could be brought to support the entire measure, and so it failed in the Senate on the last day of July.

This proved to be only a temporary setback. The individual measures were reintroduced as separate bills by Senator Stephen A. Douglas of Illinois, a Democrat. All moved quickly through the Senate and passed by large majorities. The final piece of the compromise was approved on September 8, 1850.

Perhaps the most controversial aspect of the Compromise of 1850 was the Fugitive Slave Act. The problem with this law was that it offended almost every American notion of fairness. A slave owner could claim any black person was a runaway slave by simply swearing out an *affidavit* to that effect before a special federal commissioner. Those accused of being runaways had no right to legal representation and no right to present evidence to prove their free

This poster from the 1848 presidential election pictures Zachary Taylor (left) and his vice presidential running mate, Millard Fillmore. As president, Taylor opposed the Compromise of 1850—but he died suddenly in July of that year. After succeeding to the presidency, Fillmore signed into law the Fugitive Slave Act and other elements of the compromise.

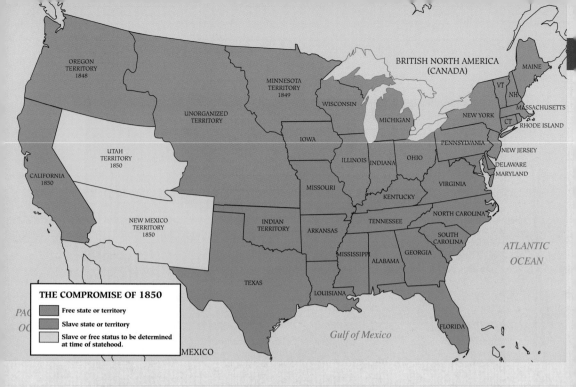

THE COMPROMISE OF 1850

- Free state or territory
- Slave state or territory
- Slave or free status to be determined at time of statehood.

status. Interference with the proceedings was a federal offense, punishable by large fines and stiff prison sentences.

The extreme nature of the law was no doubt a response to efforts in some Northern states to block attempts by Southerners to recover runaways. But the 1850 law went too far, sparking a serious backlash. Northerners who previously had not cared much about the slavery issue now began to see evidence of the insidious "slave power"—the political domination of the slaveholding class—that anti-slavery politicians and abolitionists had been complaining about. This led to the enactment of "personal liberty laws" in several Northern states. These were attempts to invoke the idea of nullification to prevent the enforcement of the Fugitive Slave Act.

The passage of the personal liberty laws lent credence to the claim by the Southern fire-eaters that Northerners could not be trusted to protect "Southern rights" (often a code phrase for "slavery"). When the time came to justify *secession*, the interference with the return of fugitive slaves would loom large in the minds of the secessionists.

In the end, the Compromise of 1850 proved to be a failure. It was offered to settle the festering disputes over slavery, but it left everyone with bitter regrets for having given in on crucial issues. Northerners came to despise the Fugitive Slave Act, which was rigged in favor of the slaveholder. Southerners lamented the loss of California, both in terms of political power and in terms of expanding Southern institutions.

The argument itself had revealed deep cracks in both of the major political parties, especially the Whigs. Within a few years, another sectional crisis would sound the death knell for the Whigs and lead to the creation of a new political party founded on anti-slavery principles: the Republican Party.

KANSAS A FREE STATE.

Squatter Sovereignty

VINDICATED!

NO WHITE SLAVERY!

The Squatters of Kansas who are favorable to **FREEDOM OF SPEECH** on all subjects which interest them, and an unmuzzled **PRESS**: who are determined to do their own **THINKING** and **VOTING** independent of **FOREIGN DICTATION**, are requested to assemble in

MASS MEETING

at the time and places following to wit:

The following speakers will be in attendance, who will address you on the important questions now before the people of Kansas.

At Fish's Store	on Monday	September	24th	at 2 o'clock P. M.	Lane	Saturday	Oct.	6th	at 2 o'clock P. M.
" Fort Scott	" Friday	"	28th	1 " "	" Scott's Town	"	September	29th	1 " "
" Stockton's Store, Little Sugar Creek	Sat.	"	29th	1 " "	" Hampden	Monday	Oct.	1st	2 " "
" Elijah Tucker's, Big	" Monday	Oct.	1st	2 " "	" Neosho, at H. Smith's Store	Tuesday	"	2d	2 " "
" Osawatomie,	Tuesday	"	2d	1 " "	" Columbia	Wednesday	"	3d	1 " "
" Mr. Partridge's, Pottowatomie Creek	Wed.	"	3d	2 " "	" Palmyra	Friday	"	5th	2 " "
" Baptist Peoria	Thursday	"	4th	2 " "	" Blanton	Saturday	"	6th	2 " "
" Springfield	Friday	"	5th	2 " "					

DR. CHAS. ROBINSON,

J. A. Wakefield, C. K. Holliday, M. F. Conway,
W. K. Vail, J. L. Speer, W. A. Ela, Josiah Miller, O. C. Brown, J. K. Goodin, Doct.
Gilpatrick, Revs. Mr. Tuton and J. E. Stewart, C. A. Foster, J. P. Fox, H. Bronson,
G. W. Brown, A. H. Malley and others.

TURN OUT AND HEAR THEM!

Ter'y Sept 24 57

The 1854 Kansas-Nebraska Act sparked a wave of violence, as slavery supporters and opponents battled for control over the territories. This poster from 1855 advertises a series of public meetings with anti-slavery leaders in Kansas.

BLEEDING KANSAS

The Compromise of 1850 kept the sectional peace for about four years. It should be acknowledged that enforcement of the Fugitive Slave Act did occasionally lead to trouble. And the appearance of Harriet Beecher Stowe's anti-slavery novel *Uncle Tom's Cabin* began to change the opinions of some Northerners. Still, on the political stage, sectional discord was subdued.

THE KANSAS-NEBRASKA ACT

The relative calm came to an abrupt end in 1854. On January 4, Senator Stephen A. Douglas of Illinois introduced the Kansas-Nebraska Act. The bill would open up the Kansas and Nebraska territories for settlement. Douglas's bill would permit residents of the territories to decide for themselves whether they wanted to become slave or free states. This idea became known as *popular sovereignty*.

There was no need to have said anything about slavery in the two territories. Both Kansas and Nebraska were north of the 36°30´ line, so under the Missouri Compromise both would be free states. The bill would essentially destroy the Missouri Compromise by offering the South the possibility of creating new slave states. Douglas's reason for doing this was political. He wanted to run for president, but he needed Southern support to secure the Democratic nomination. Because of his involvement with the Compromise of 1850, Douglas was not popular within the Southern wing of his party. Lending support to the creation of more slave states might change this.

At first, President Franklin Pierce, a Democrat, opposed the Kansas-Nebraska Act. He did not want to reopen the slavery issue. But a group of slave state senators—along with Pierce's secretary of war, Jefferson Davis of Mississippi—made it clear that if Pierce refused to support the repeal of the Missouri Compromise, the South would oppose him. In the end, the president not only endorsed the Kansas bill but also promised to make it a test of party loyalty.

Harriet Beecher Stowe (1811–1896) gained national attention after writing a novel about slave life, *Uncle Tom's Cabin*. Stowe was angry about the 1850 Fugitive Slave Act, and she wrote the book in response. It was originally serialized in an abolitionist newspaper during 1851; the novel was published in 1852. *Uncle Tom's Cabin* made an enormous impression on Northern public opinion by presenting enslaved characters as human and dramatizing the abuses heaped upon them by harsh masters.

Northern opinion was bitterly opposed to the act, but Douglas and the Democratic Party rammed the bill through both houses of Congress in relatively quick order. Having decided the question in haste, the nation could now repent at leisure.

BLOOD ON THE PRAIRIE

The Kansas-Nebraska Act destroyed the Whig Party. The forceful opposition of Northern Whigs to the bill completely drove the Southern wing of the party away. In time, Northern Whigs would unite with the fledgling Free-Soil Party and Democrats who had opposed the bill to create the Republican Party.

Another consequence of the Kansas-Nebraska Act was the outbreak of open warfare on the Kansas prairie. The name by which this period would become known hinted at the violence: "Bleeding Kansas."

Because the citizens of the territories would decide the slavery question, both the Free-Soil and pro-slavery sides encouraged settlement by people who supported their views. The New England Emigrant Aid Society, an abolitionist group, got started first and earned a lot of publicity. But the majority of Kansas settlers came from the Ohio Valley. Most of them also wanted to make Kansas a free state.

They had trouble getting their way, however. "Border Ruffians" crossed over from Missouri on Election Day to increase the ranks of pro-slavery voters. They also tried to intimidate Free-Soil settlers and keep them from voting. As a result, Kansas initially elected a pro-slavery delegate to Congress and a pro-slavery territorial legislature. However, later investigation would reveal that, out of 5,247 pro-slavery ballots cast in the legislative election, 4,968 were fraudulent. Despite this, the territorial governor refused to call a new election, and the bogus legislature passed a slave code, permitted only pro-slavery men to hold public offices, and made it a crime even to question the legality of slavery in Kansas.

The Free-Soil element in the state organized its own government, with its capital in Topeka. Kansas now had two territorial governments, one of which was recognized as legitimate by the president and the Senate, the other by the House of Representatives. When the governor finally decided that the Free-Soil government was more legitimate, he was dismissed by President Pierce and replaced by a pro-slavery man.

Violence finally erupted. On May 21, 1856, about 700 pro-slavery men rode into the free-state

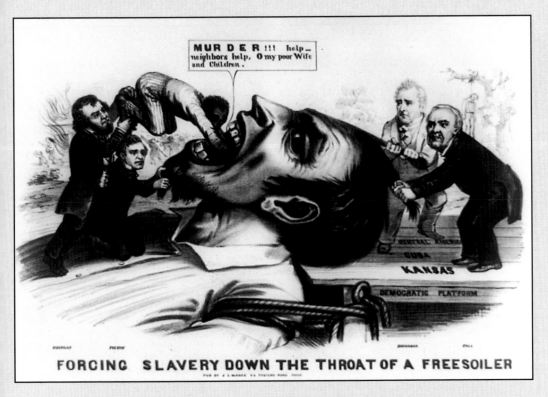

FORCING SLAVERY DOWN THE THROAT OF A FREESOILER

This newspaper cartoon from 1856 blames Democratic leaders (including Franklin Pierce, James Buchanan, and Stephen A. Douglas) for the violence in Kansas.

stronghold of Lawrence and sacked the town. Partly in response to this event, someone—only later would the name John Brown be associated with this act—led a group of Free-Soilers into the bottomlands along Pottawatomie Creek, taking five pro-slavery men from their homes and splitting their skulls open with swords. For the next four months, open warfare raged across the prairie.

POLITICAL CONSEQUENCES

Some would say the fighting had already come to Washington. Just before the Lawrence affair, Senator Charles Sumner of Massachusetts had delivered a two-day speech titled "The Crime Against Kansas," in which he had verbally attacked Senator Andrew Butler of South Carolina, as well as other Southern leaders. On May 22, Butler's cousin, Congressman Preston Brooks, approached Sumner at his desk on the floor of the Senate and beat him senseless with a cane. The attack, celebrated in the South and reviled in the North, revealed the acrimony that was affecting the entire nation.

The Kansas-Nebraska Act proved extremely unpopular in the North. Only 7 out of 54 Democrats from the North who had voted for the act won reelection, and many of those who had opposed it were willing to end their association with a party that had made such an act a test of loyalty. These men found common cause with the Northern Whigs and the smaller Free-Soil and Liberty parties. Soon, these groups coalesced into the Republican Party. One result of this defection by Northern Democrats was that the Democratic Party became increasingly a sectional party, beholden to the South.

The Republican Party experienced quick success across the North. Former Whigs or Democrats who joined the party, such as Salmon P. Chase of Ohio and William H. Seward of New York, gave the party legitimacy and political power. Although the Republicans adopted many of the Whigs' political ideas, opposition to slavery was their fundamental issue. In 1856, the Republican nominee for president, John C. Frémont of California, came within 60 electoral votes of winning the office.

The new president, James Buchanan, tried to have Kansas admitted to the Union as a slave state in 1857. However, this effort was blocked in Congress. When a new vote was held in the territory, Kansans voted overwhelmingly to reject the pro-slavery Lecompton Constitution and create an anti-slavery government. Kansas would ultimately be admitted to the Union as a free state in 1861.

339.

FRANK LESLIE'S
ILLUSTRATED
NEWSPAPER

Entered according to Act of Congress, in the year 1857, by Frank Leslie, in the Clerk's Office of the District Court for the Southern District of New York. (Copyrighted June 22, 1857.)

No. 82.—VOL. IV.]   **NEW YORK, SATURDAY, JUNE 27, 1857.**   [PRICE 6 CENTS.

TO TOURISTS AND TRAVELLERS.

We shall be happy to receive personal narratives, of land or sea, including adventures and incidents, from every person who pleases to correspond with our paper.

We take this opportunity of returning our thanks to our numerous artistic correspondents throughout the country, for the many sketches we are constantly receiving from them of the news of the day. We trust they will spare no pains to furnish us with drawings of events as they may occur. We would also remind them that it is necessary to send all sketches, if possible, by the earliest conveyance.

VISIT TO DRED SCOTT—HIS FAMILY—INCIDENTS OF HIS LIFE—DECISION OF THE SUPREME COURT.

WHILE standing in the Fair grounds at St. Louis, and engaged in conversation with a prominent citizen of that enterprising city, he suddenly asked us if we would not like to be introduced to Dred Scott. Upon expressing a desire to be thus honored, the gentleman called to an old negro who was standing near by, and our wish was gratified. Dred made a rude obeisance to our recognition, and seemed to enjoy the notice we expended upon him. We found him on examination to be a pure-blooded African, perhaps fifty years of age, with a shrewd, intelligent, good-natured face, of rather light frame, being not more than five feet six inches high. After some general remarks we expressed a wish to get his portrait (we had made efforts before, through correspondents, and failed, and asked him if he would not go to Fitzgibbon's gallery and

ELIZA AND LIZZIE, CHILDREN OF DRED SCOTT.

have it taken. The gentleman present explained to Dred that it was proper he should have his likeness in the "great illustrated paper of the country," overruled his many objections, which seemed to grow out of a superstitious feeling, and he promised to be at the gallery the next day. This appointment Dred did not keep. Determined not to be foiled, we sought an interview with Mr. Crane, Dred's lawyer, who promptly gave us a letter of introduction, explaining to Dred that it was to his advantage to have his picture taken to be engraved for our paper, and also directions where we could find his domicile. We found the place with difficulty, the streets in Dred's neighborhood being more closely defined in the plan of the city than on the mother earth; we finally reached a wooden house, however, protected by a balcony that answered the description. Approaching the door, we saw a smart, tidy-looking negress, perhaps thirty years of age, who, with two female assistants, was busy ironing. To our question, "Is this where Dred Scott lives?" we received, rather hesitatingly, the answer, "Yes." Upon our asking if he was home, she said,

"What white man acts dad nigger for!—why don't white man 'tend to his own business, and let dat nigger 'lone! Some of dese days dey'll steal dot nigger—dat are a fact."

own business, and let dot nigger 'lone! Some of dese days dey'll steal dot nigger—dat are a fact."

DRED SCOTT. PHOTOGRAPHED BY FITZGIBBON, OF ST. LOUIS.   HIS WIFE, HARRIET. PHOTOGRAPHED BY FITZGIBBON, OF ST. LOUIS.

DEEPENING DIVISIONS

I n the first 68 years of its history, the Supreme Court only once struck down a law as ***unconstitutional***. The second time came in 1857, in a case involving a slave who had sued for his freedom. The controversial decision in that case would be a major factor in the deepening sectional crisis.

DRED SCOTT V. SANDFORD

Dred Scott was a slave who eventually came to be owned by Dr. John Emerson, an army surgeon. From 1830 to 1842, Emerson served in a number of places, including posts in Illinois, a free state, and in Minnesota Territory, which had been declared "free territory" by the Missouri Compromise. Dred Scott accompanied the doctor to his assigned posts. Three years after Emerson's death in 1843, Scott and his wife sued Emerson's widow for their freedom, claiming that their being taken to Illinois and Minnesota Territory had released them from bondage. The Scotts were successful in the lower state courts, but in 1852 they lost on appeal to the Missouri Supreme Court.

The Scotts then launched another lawsuit, this time in the federal court system. They were able to do this because Mrs. Emerson's brother, John Sanford, had assumed legal responsibility for Dr. Emerson's estate, which included the Scott family. The case finally reached the U.S. Supreme Court in 1855.

The Court's decision in *Dred Scott v. Sandford*—John Sanford's name had been misspelled in court papers—was written by Chief Justice Roger Taney of Maryland, a former slaveholder. He declared that a black person could not be a citizen in the sense meant by the framers of the U.S. Constitution. Thus blacks were not entitled to the rights and protections afforded to citizens. This should have been the end of the matter, as it would mean Dred Scott had no standing to sue. But Taney went further, declaring that the Missouri Compromise had been unconstitutional and that Congress had no authority to legislate against slavery in the territories.

A few days after President James Buchanan's inauguration in 1857, Chief Justice Roger Taney (1777–1864) handed down the decision in *Dred Scott v. Sandford*. Taney declared the Missouri Compromise unconstitutional, writing that Congress did not have the authority to forbid slavery in U.S. territories.

Politically, the Dred Scott decision was a lot like the Kansas-Nebraska Act—something done to settle the slavery question that instead merely inflamed it. The Republican Party was able to use the Dred Scott case to support its claims that a Southern "slave power" was exerting influence over national affairs for sectional gain.

DEBATING THE ISSUES

The 1850s had seen the steady rise of Stephen A. Douglas of Illinois as a nationally prominent figure. It was expected that Douglas would seek the Democratic presidential nomination in 1860. First, however, he had to win reelection to the Senate in 1858.

But Douglas was vulnerable in that race. The Kansas-Nebraska Act was unpopular, and Republicans felt they had a good opportunity to capture the Illinois legislature in 1858. This would mean the defeat of Douglas, because senators were elected by state legislatures at the time. In an unprecedented move, the Illinois Republican Party met in mid-June and announced that if Republicans won control of the state legislature, they would elect Abraham Lincoln to replace Douglas as senator.

Although Lincoln was not as well known as Douglas, he was not a surprise choice. A former Whig, he had served a term in Congress, then resumed his law practice after leaving office in 1849. But the Kansas-Nebraska Act had spurred him to return to politics. He had helped form the Illinois Republican Party and worked hard to defeat Democratic candidates.

Lincoln proposed a series of debates, and Douglas eventually agreed to appear with him in seven Illinois congressional districts. One man would open with an hour-long speech, to which his opponent could reply for an hour and a half, followed by a 30-minute rebuttal from the first speaker. Slavery was virtually the only theme of the debates.

In his speeches, Douglas tried to paint Lincoln as an extremist on the slavery and race issues, forcing the challenger on the defensive. Sometimes this worked and sometimes it did not.

Lincoln scored some important points. He was able to maneuver Douglas into stating that his policy of popular sovereignty "contemplates that [slavery] shall last forever." But his rhetorical high point was appropriately saved for the final debate. Summarizing the entire series of debates, he characterized the issues between himself and Douglas as a conflict

> on the part of one class that looks upon the institution of slavery as a wrong, and of another class that does not look upon it as a wrong. That is the issue that will continue in this country when these poor tongues of Judge Douglas and myself shall be silent. It is the eternal struggle between these two principles—right and wrong—throughout the world. They are the two principles that have stood face to face from the beginning of time; and will ever continue to struggle. The one is the common right of humanity and the other the divine right of kings.

When the election ended, the Democrats had retained control of the legislature. They reelected Douglas to the Senate. But statewide, the Republicans had polled more votes than the Democrats. And Lincoln's strong showing had made him something of a name in national Republican circles, even in defeat. That name would be remembered two years later.

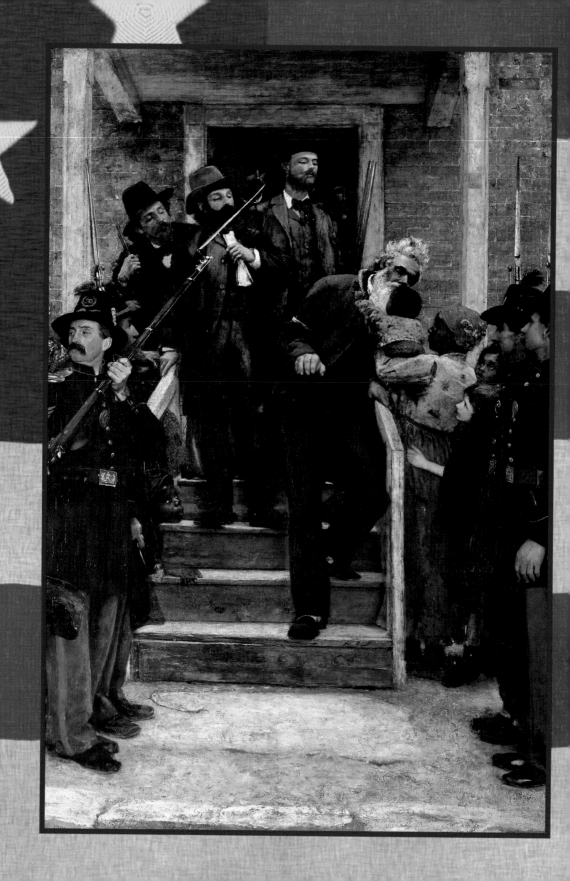

In this idealized painting, titled *The Last Moments of John Brown*, the anti-slavery firebrand kisses a black child on the way to his execution for leading an October 1859 raid on the federal arsenal at Harpers Ferry, Virginia. Many Northern abolitionists came to regard Brown as a martyr, while Southerners considered him a dangerous fanatic.

5

THE ELECTION OF 1860

On the night of October 16, 1859, John Brown led a motley collection of 21 men into Harpers Ferry, Virginia. His intention was to seize the federal armory there and then incite a widespread slave revolt. This poorly conceived plan was defeated barely 36 hours later, and Brown was hanged on December 2.

But Brown's act had created alarm throughout the slave states. Papers and maps he was carrying when captured pointed to the possibility of a wider conspiracy that might strike in other states.

Although most Northerners condemned Brown's violent actions, some abolitionists considered him a martyr for their cause. The poet and essayist Ralph

Waldo Emerson commented that Brown would "make the gallows as glorious as the cross." In the view of Southerners, however, the abolitionists were praising a man who would have set loose the slaves to slit the throats of their children in the night. The fire-eaters accused Republicans of sympathy for Brown, and they were quick to take advantage of the fear incited by the Harpers Ferry raid.

THE PRESIDENTIAL CAMPAIGN

In January 1860, the Alabama Democratic Party adopted what became known as the Alabama Platform. This set of resolutions required Alabama's delegation to the Democratic convention to insist that the party's nominee commit to a congressional slave code that would protect slavery in all territories prior to statehood. If the national party disagreed, the delegates were to walk out of the convention. More than any other single act of the year, this set the nation on the road to secession and civil war.

The Democrats held their presidential nominating convention in Charleston, South Carolina, in late April. When the convention adopted a platform that did not include a call for a territorial slave code, about 50 of the Southern delegates walked out. However, although the fire-eaters had lost the vote on the slave code, they had thrown the Democratic Party into dis-array. Douglas could not get enough votes to win the party's nomination. After 57 fruitless ballots, the convention shifted to Baltimore.

The second convention was no more harmonious than the first. The Southern delegates who had left Charleston sought readmission, but the Douglas supporters had organized rival delegations to replace them. Once again, the Deep South walked out, this time for good. Douglas was soon nominated as the Democratic Party's candidate at the Baltimore

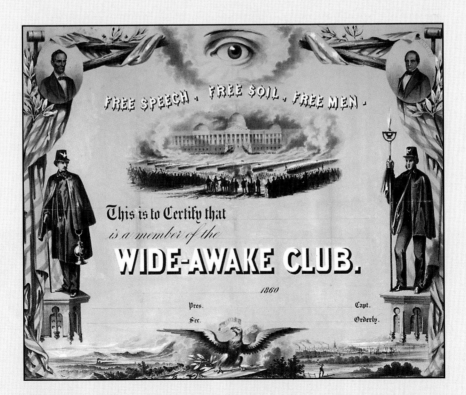

A membership certificate for the Wide-Awake Club, a Republican organization formed during the 1860 election campaign.

convention. The Southern Democrats held an alternate convention in Richmond, Virginia. They chose John C. Breckenridge of Kentucky as their presidential candidate.

In May the Republicans met in Chicago. Unlike the Democrats, they needed just three ballots to choose their candidate: Abraham Lincoln.

A FOUR-WAY RACE

In addition to Lincoln, Douglas, and Breckenridge, there was a fourth presidential candidate. The Constitutional Union Party, formed in 1860 and made up of former Whigs who had not become Republicans, put forward John Bell of Tennessee. However, Douglas was the only candidate with a chance to gain significant numbers of votes all across the country. Lincoln was not even on the ballot in the South, and Breckenridge would get few votes in the North.

Bell

Breckenridge

Douglas

Lincoln

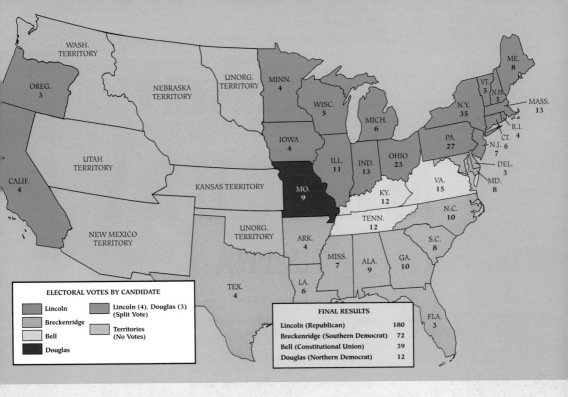

ELECTORAL VOTES BY CANDIDATE

- Lincoln
- Breckenridge
- Bell
- Douglas
- Lincoln (4), Douglas (3) (Split Vote)
- Territories (No Votes)

FINAL RESULTS	
Lincoln (Republican)	180
Breckenridge (Southern Democrat)	72
Bell (Constitutional Union)	39
Douglas (Northern Democrat)	12

When the election was held, Lincoln outpolled the other candidates. He received about 40 percent of the popular vote and won the electoral vote decisively.

During the campaign, Lincoln had explained that he would not attempt to abolish slavery, just prevent it from spreading. He also promised to enforce the Fugitive Slave Act and other laws. However, the Republicans also promised to implement new tariffs protecting Northern industries.

Southerners saw Lincoln's election as further proof that their influence over national politics was weakening. Despite not carrying a single Southern state, Lincoln had been elected easily. Many Southern leaders began to argue that breaking away from the Union was the only way to preserve their society.

CHARLESTON

MERCURY

EXTRA:

Passed unanimously at 1.15 o'clock, P. M. December 20th, 1860.

AN ORDINANCE

To dissolve the Union between the State of South Carolina and other States united with her under the compact entitled " The Constitution of the United States of America."

We, the People of the State of South Carolina, in Convention assembled, do declare and ordain, and it is hereby declared and ordained,

That the Ordinance adopted by us in Convention, on the twenty-third day of May, in the year of our Lord one thousand seven hundred and eighty-eight, whereby the Constitution of the United States of America was ratified, and also, all Acts and parts of Acts of the General Assembly of this State, ratifying amendments of the said Constitution, are hereby repealed; and that the union now subsisting between South Carolina and other States, under the name of " The United States of America," is hereby dissolved.

THE

UNION

IS

DISSOLVED!

The front page of the *Charleston Mercury* from December 20, 1860, reprints an ordinance of secession passed unanimously by a convention of South Carolina leaders. South Carolina was the first state to secede; other Southern states quickly followed.

6

SECESSION AND WAR

Secession was not a new idea in 1860. The Southern leadership had threatened secession in 1850, over the admission of California to the Union, but they had not followed through with this threat. The threat of secession was repeated during the 1856 and 1860 elections. Both times, Southern leaders declared that they would not tolerate a Republican president.

THE SOUTH TAKES ACTION

With Lincoln's electoral victory an accomplished fact, everyone expected South Carolina to take the first step. On November 9, just three days after the election, the South Carolina legislature passed a resolution calling for the creation of a statewide secession convention. Ominously, the legislature also authorized the governor to spend $100,000 for arms.

Delegates to the convention quickly passed an ordinance of secession, declaring South Carolina out of the Union on December 20, 1860. With the first step taken, the other cotton states soon followed. Mississippi seceded on January 9, 1861; Florida on January 10; Alabama on the 11th; Georgia on the 19th; Louisiana on the 26th; and Texas on February 1. In several of these states, local militia or armed mobs seized federal facilities and property before the act of secession had been passed.

NO SOLUTIONS TO BE FOUND

The Buchanan administration did not react to this crisis. Although the president firmly believed that secession was not legal, he also believed that the federal government had no power to oppose secession.

In Congress, attempts were made to settle the emerging crisis by compromise. The most prominent effort was that put forward by Senator John J. Crittenden of Kentucky. Crittenden's proposal would essentially have enshrined the Missouri Compromise in a series of constitutional amendments that could not themselves be changed at some future

An illustrated newspaper article about the secession meetings in South Carolina, December 1860.

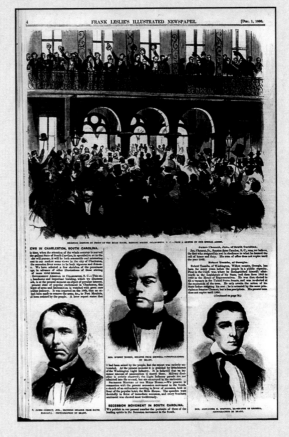

time. Lincoln opposed the Crittenden plan. He believed it would give away all that had been won in the election and that it would result in Southern demands for new slave states. Crittenden's proposal, along with other compromise plans offered in Congress, failed to get off the ground.

In February 1861, delegates from a scattering of states attended the Washington Peace Conference in the nation's capital. The Virginia legislature had suggested the conference to find a peaceful solution to the sectional rift. But the proposal put forward by the conference differed little from other plans, and in any case it came too late to do much good.

Meanwhile, secessionist leaders were able to create their new nation—the Confederate States of America—in slightly more than three months' time. Most of the work came in an incredibly brief period during February. Delegates from six Southern states gathered at a convention in Montgomery, Alabama, on February 4, 1861. (Texas did not attend, having not yet finished its secession process.) By the 8th, they had adopted a constitution, on the 9th they chose a provisional president (Jefferson Davis) and vice president (Alexander Stephens), and by the 18th they had inaugurated their government.

Just over two weeks later, Abraham Lincoln was sworn in as the 16th president of the United States. There now existed two governments where once there had been only one. Although both governments claimed peaceful intentions, both were willing to risk war to establish the primacy of their point of view.

THE FORT SUMTER CRISIS

Even before South Carolina's secession, it was clear that the federal facilities in Charleston Harbor would be a point of friction between the secessionists and the federal government. The day after Lincoln's election, Lieutenant Colonel John Gardner, the commander of the U.S. troops in the harbor forts, tried to transfer some munitions from the Charleston arsenal to the forts themselves. He was blocked by a mob.

The federal soldiers were stationed in several facilities. Most of the soldiers—about 70 officers and men—were at Fort Moultrie on Sullivan's Island, guarding the northern side of the harbor. A few officers and about 100 civilian workmen were at incomplete Fort Sumter, in the middle of the harbor. One ordnance sergeant was stationed at Castle Pinkney, close to the city itself.

After the November incident, Gardner was replaced by Major Robert Anderson. Although Anderson immediately asked for reinforcements, Southerners in Buchanan's cabinet persuaded the president not to send more troops. Instead they made an arrangement by which South Carolina promised that national property in Charleston would not be seized. Nonetheless, Anderson continued to request help to hold his position.

On the night of December 26, Anderson and his troops evacuated Fort Moultrie and occupied Fort Sumter in the middle of Charleston Harbor. South Carolinians were angry, believing their arrangement with Buchanan had been violated. Southern delegates

A watercolor painting shows soldiers at their posts in Fort Moultrie, Charleston, South Carolina. In the distance, an American flag flies over Fort Sumter.

met with the president and insisted that he order Anderson to return to Fort Moultrie.

After some debate within his cabinet, President Buchanan decided to hold Fort Sumter. On January 5, the steamship *Star of the West* set sail from New York on a supposedly secret mission to transport supplies and 200 soldiers to reinforce Major Anderson. But South Carolinians were alerted to the relief expedition, and shore batteries fired on the steamer at the entrance to Charleston Harbor on January 9. The ship was forced to turn away.

On February 15, the new Confederate Congress resolved that the Southern states should immediately take possession of Fort Sumter and another federal fort in Florida, Fort Pickens. If negotiations for the forts failed, the Confederate president was authorized to use force to capture the forts.

Southern newspapers, meanwhile, urged an attack on federal forts in order to stave off the prospect of reconciliation with the Union. "We are in danger," the *Charleston Mercury* opined, "of being dragged back eventually to the old political affiliation with the states and people from whom we have just cut loose." One Alabamian told the Confederate secretary of war, "Unless you sprinkle blood in the face of the people of Alabama, they will be back in the old Union in less than ten days!"

Moreover, it was an article of faith in the South that the opening of hostilities would bring over Virginia and Maryland to the Confederacy, and at the same time Jefferson Davis was being advised (by former president Franklin Pierce) that the Democrats of the North would stand together with the Democrats of the South instead of the Republicans. Thus, action against Sumter would not provoke a war, according to this thinking. It would in fact prevent one, by giving Lincoln second thoughts.

With Lincoln's inauguration on March 4, the problem of secession became his to solve. One of the first official messages to land on the new president's desk was the news from Major Anderson that Sumter's provisions would not last much longer. Getting additional provisions into the fort became a top priority. In April, a federal fleet left New York on a mission to resupply Fort Sumter.

OPENING SHOTS OF THE WAR

On April 10, before the fleet could arrive, Confederate leaders decided to attack Fort Sumter. Shortly after noon the next day, Confederate general P. G. T. Beauregard demanded that Anderson surrender his post. When Anderson refused, Beauregard ordered the Confederate batteries to fire on Fort Sumter the following morning. The first guns opened up at about 4:30 A.M.

The federal soldiers did not stand much of a chance of successfully defending the post. Not enough guns were mounted, and most of the heaviest guns were in exposed positions. Plus, Anderson did not have enough men to properly manage even a few of the guns. Anderson did not even try to return fire until daylight. The bombardment eventually started a fire that threatened the room where Fort Sumter's gunpowder was stored. This prompted Anderson to give the order to strike the flag during the afternoon of April 13. There had been no casualties on either side, a curious beginning to the bloodiest war in American history.

The news of the bombardment and surrender of Fort Sumter had a number of predictable effects. Wild celebrations filled the streets of Richmond on April 13, and a crowd took down the American flag from the capitol and ran up in its place the newly designed Stars and Bars. Similar events occurred in Nashville, Tennessee, as well as Wilmington, Raleigh, and Goldsboro, North Carolina. Lincoln issued a call for troops to put down the rebellion on April 15, and the Civil War was under way. Four more states—Virginia, Tennessee, North Carolina, and Arkansas—would secede in response to this call for troops.

* * * * *

There is a sad epilogue to the events at Charleston. Almost exactly four years later, Robert Anderson would return to Fort Sumter to raise the very same flag he had hauled down at the start of the war. After this ceremony there was a banquet, and Anderson was asked to make a toast. He raised his glass to "the good, the great, the honest man, Abraham Lincoln"—who at that very moment was in the presidential box at Ford's Theatre. It was there on April 14, 1865, that the president was mortally wounded by an assassin's bullet.

1787	Delegates to the Constitutional Convention agree to allow Congress to end the slave trade in 1808; Congress passes the Northwest Ordinance, which bans slavery in all territory north of the Ohio River and west of the Appalachian Mountains.
1794	Eli Whitney patents the cotton gin, a machine for removing the seeds from cotton fiber; the device will make cotton cultivation highly profitable and thus increase the demand for slave labor on cotton plantations throughout the South.
1820	Congress passes the Missouri Compromise, by which Maine is partitioned from Massachusetts and admitted to the Union as a free state, Missouri is admitted as a slave state, and it is decided that all lands in the former Louisiana Territory north of latitude 36°30' will be free.
1828	High tariffs on imported goods spur discontent in the South.
1831	Nat Turner's slave revolt occurs in Southampton County, Virginia.
1832	In November, South Carolina enacts an "ordinance of nullification." Only the introduction of a compromise tariff level averts a showdown with the federal government.
1836	Texans win independence from Mexico.
1845	The United States annexes Texas and admits it to the Union as a slave state.
1846	The Mexican War begins.
1848	The United States wins the Mexican War, forcing Mexico to cede a vast territory that will become the future states of California, Nevada, Utah, Arizona, and New Mexico.

1850	The Compromise of 1850 is passed; its components include admission of California to the Union as a free state and passage of the Fugitive Slave Act.
1852	*Uncle Tom's Cabin*, by Harriet Beecher Stowe, is published.
1854	The passage of the Kansas-Nebraska Act introduces popular sovereignty as a way to determine whether a new territory will have slavery; in Kansas this leads to violence between pro- and anti-slavery elements.
1856	James Buchanan is elected president.
1857	The Supreme Court hands down the Dred Scott decision, which rules the Missouri Compromise unconstitutional.
1858	The Lincoln-Douglas debates, held during the senatorial campaign in Illinois, attract national attention.
1860	Abraham Lincoln, a Republican, is elected president; on December 20, South Carolina secedes from the Union.
1861	Mississippi, Florida, Alabama, Georgia, and Louisiana secede in January, and Texas secedes on February 1; the Confederate States of America passes a constitution, selects a provisional president and vice president, and inaugurates its government between February 8 and 18; Lincoln is inaugurated on March 4; on April 12, Confederate batteries begin bombarding Fort Sumter in Charleston Harbor; on April 15, President Lincoln issues a call for soldiers to put down the South's insurrection.

GLOSSARY

ABOLITION—the outlawing or banning of slavery.

ABOLITIONIST—relating to or concerning a movement whose goal was to end slavery; a person who advocated the outlawing of slavery.

AFFIDAVIT—a sworn, written statement made before a government or court official.

ANNEX—to take possession of and incorporate a territory into a larger or more powerful state.

CASH CROP—a crop (such as cotton or tobacco) produced primarily for sale at market.

CEDE—to yield or transfer control of a territory to another government.

EMANCIPATION—the act of freeing; specifically, the freeing of slaves.

FIRE-EATER—a Southerner who was vehemently opposed to any restrictions on slavery.

FREE-SOILER—someone who opposed extending slavery to new territories or admitting any more slave states to the Union, but who was willing to accept slavery where it already existed.

NULLIFICATION—the action of a state attempting to prevent the operation or enforcement of a U.S. law within its territory.

POPULAR SOVEREIGNTY—the idea that the people living in a newly organized territory had the right to decide by a vote whether or not there would be slavery in the territory.

SECEDE—to withdraw from a political union.

SECESSION—the act of withdrawing from a political union.

TARIFF—a tax imposed on imported goods.

UNCONSTITUTIONAL—not consistent with the U.S. Constitution and therefore unlawful.

BOOKS FOR STUDENTS:

Anderson, Dale. *The Causes of the Civil War*. Cleveland: World Almanac Library, 2004.

Armstrong, Jennifer. *Photo by Brady: A Picture of the Civil War*. New York: Atheneum Books, 2005.

January, Brendan. *The Dred Scott Decision*. Danbury, Conn.: Children's Press, 1998.

McArthur, Debra. *The Kansas-Nebraska Act and "Bleeding Kansas" in American History*. Berkeley Heights, N.J.: Enslow Publishers, 2003.

Naden, Corinne J., and Rose Blue. *Why Fight? The Causes of the American Civil War*. Chicago: Raintree, 1999.

BOOKS FOR OLDER READERS:

Ayers, Edward L. *What Caused the Civil War? Reflections on the South and Southern History*. New York: W. W. Norton, 2005.

Catton, William, and Bruce Catton. *Two Roads to Sumter: Abraham Lincoln, Jefferson Davis, and the March to the Civil War*. New York: Sterling Publishing, 2001.

Current, Richard. *Lincoln and the First Shot*. Long Grove, Ill.: Waveland Press, 1990.

Donald, David Herbert. *Lincoln*. New York: Simon & Schuster, 1995.

Freehling, William. *Prelude to Civil War: The Nullification Controversy in South Carolina, 1816–1836*. New York: Oxford University Press, 1992.

McPherson, James. *Battle Cry of Freedom: The Civil War Era*. New York: Oxford University Press, 1988.

INTERNET RESOURCES

HTTP://MEMBERS.AOL.COM/JFEPPERSON/CAUSES.HTML

This site, maintained by the author, includes documents and links.

HTTP://WWW.PBS.ORG/CIVILWAR

The companion website to Ken Burns's award-winning PBS documentary *The Civil War.*

HTTP://WWW.NATIONALCIVILWARMUSEUM.ORG

Website for the National Civil War Museum.

HTTP://WWW.PBS.ORG/WGBH/AMEX/BROWN/

Home page for the PBS film *John Brown's Holy War*, about the infamous abolitionist.

HTTP://BIOGUIDE.CONGRESS.GOV

Students can use this site provided by the U.S. Congress to find biographies of important government leaders like Henry Clay and John C. Calhoun.

HTTP://WWW.CWC.LSU.EDU

The United States Civil War Center provides an index of information about the Civil War available on the Internet.

HTTP://WWW.PBS.ORG/WNET/AAWORLD/

The PBS program *African American World* presents a great deal of information about slavery in America, as well as the many contributions of blacks in U.S. history.

Publisher's Note: The websites listed on this page were active at the time of publication. The publisher is not responsible for websites that have changed their address or discontinued operation since the date of publication.

Numbers in **bold italics** refer to captions.

PICTURE CREDITS

Page
2:      Library of Congress
7:      National Archives; Library
        of Congress; Library of Con-
        gress
8:      National Archives
8-9:   National Archives
11:     Independence National
        Historical Park
13:     North Wind Picture Archives
14:     © OTTN Publishing
18:     Library of Congress
18-19: U.S. Senate Collection
21:     North Wind Picture Archives
25:     Library of Congress
26:     © OTTN Publishing
28:     Kansas State Historical
        Society
31:     National Archives
33:     Library of Congress
36:     Library of Congress
39:     Library of Congress
42:     Thomas Hovenden, "The
        Last Moments of John
        Brown," 1882-84. The Met-
        ropolitan Museum of Art,
        gift of Mr. and Mrs. Carl
        Stoeckel, 1897 (97.5). Pho-
        tograph © 1982 the Metro-
        politan Museum of Art.
45:     Library of Congress
46:     Library of Congress; Library
        of Congress; Library of Con-
        gress; National Archives
47:     © OTTN Publishing
48:     MPI/Getty Images
51:     Library of Congress
54:     Library of Congress

Front Cover: Library of Congress (top); Library of Congress (inset)
Back Cover: National Archives

ABOUT THE AUTHOR

JAMES F. EPPERSON is a 50-something mathematician with a life-long interest in the Civil War. Raised in western Kentucky, educated at the University of Michigan and Carnegie-Mellon University, he has worked as a university mathematics teacher in Georgia, Alabama, and now Michigan, where he is currently employed as an editor for the American Mathematical Society. He has authored 20 journal articles in mathematics as well as a textbook published by John Wiley & Sons. His historical interests have led to the publication of two magazine articles on Civil War subjects, as well as the creation of two Civil War–related websites. Mr. Epperson lives in Ann Arbor, Michigan, with his wife, two children, and faithful Border collie, Samantha.